IMAGES
of America

CAÑON CITY

IMAGES
of America

CAÑON CITY

Anne C. Vinnola

ARCADIA
PUBLISHING

Published by Arcadia Publishing
Charleston, South Carolina

Library of Congress Control Number: 2009937654

For all general information contact Arcadia Publishing at:
Telephone 843-853-2070
Fax 843-853-0044
E-mail sales@arcadiapublishing.com
For customer service and orders:
Toll-Free 1-888-313-2665

Visit us on the Internet at www.arcadiapublishing.com

This book is dedicated to my husband, Jerry,
who supported me through the whole process;
my children Casey Maas, Kelley, Tony, and Jenny,
who have encouraged me every day;
my parents, Al and Janet Starner, who gave me a love for books;
my sister Alissa Wood, who is one of the most positive people I know;
and also my friends, who never tell me I cannot do something.
Above all, I thank God, who gives me the strength to be all I can be.

CONTENTS

ACKNOWLEDGMENTS

I wish to humbly thank the true keepers of Cañon City history, the staff of the Royal Gorge Regional History and Museum Center: Cliff Hight, Natalie Bard, Sue Cochran, Nancy Masimer, and Loretta Bailey. Without their knowledge and assistance, this book would not have been possible. I will miss the many afternoons seated at my table listening to the rich history of Cañon City being discussed and discovered by these truly dedicated friends and the wonderful volunteers who taught me much about being ever friendly and helpful.

Unless otherwise noted, all images appear courtesy of the Royal Gorge Regional Museum and History Center.

INTRODUCTION

Cañon City, the little town along the mighty Arkansas River that thought big thoughts and dreamed big dreams, is captured in this book with photographs covering the century and a half of its existence. Fascinating people and places abound, showcasing a rich and varied history.

Pioneers and their stories lead off these pages with the beginning of Colorado's large, profitable fruit and farming industries. Ranching families brought large herds of cattle and exciting rodeos to the region. Landmarks, early dinosaur discoveries, and oil wells are shown, as are the first hotels, national and local parks, and the breathtakingly famous Royal Gorge Bridge.

Religion and education played large parts in the settling of Cañon City. Several men who changed the political scene of Colorado hailed from Cañon City, as did athletes and war veterans. Ever a social community, Cañon City has conducted annual music and blossom festivals.

The business of crime claims a large part of Cañon City heritage, with the first territorial prison installed in the new town in 1871.

Cañon City was the setting for hundreds of silent films, as well as modern films of the 20th century, bringing visits by John Wayne, Slim Pickens, Charles Bronson, Goldie Hawn, George Segal, and other notables.

Coal, gold, silver, and marble mines and quarries have helped pump lifeblood into the local economy. Recovering the land's riches has led to geological finds, as well as mining wars, strikes, and disasters.

This photograph of busy Cañon City was taken looking west from the 600 block of Main Street around 1932, with the Cañon Theater (left) showing *The Red Mill* and the Fremont County National Bank farther up the block, and the Harrison and Harding buildings on the right.

One

At the Foot of the Grand Canyon of the Arkansas

Buell and Boyd, engineers who platted Denver and Pueblo, platted Cañon City to include 1,200 acres north of the Arkansas River, as well as east and west of Soda Point in early 1860. The little town was named after the Grand Canyon of the Arkansas. The Spanish spelling of Cañon City was chosen by the Smith brothers, Josiah and Stephen, who also named Pueblo. Cañon City thrived until the Civil War broke out, virtually turning it into a ghost town. After the Civil War, several families known as "Resurrectionists" saw promise in Cañon City and began to invest their time, energy, and finances into the town. Cañon City was incorporated on April 1, 1872.

William C. Catlin was born in Lincolnshire, England, in 1827 and came to find gold in the mountains surrounding Cañon City. His homestead was extensive, and it is believed that he donated the land for the Greenwood Cemetery to the city, as well as land for the first territorial prison. Catlin built one of the first cabins in Cañon City, which now sits behind the Rudd cabin at the Royal Gorge Regional Museum and History Center. Catlin opened the first brickyard, making many of the bricks used to construct several of the first buildings in Cañon City.

A distant relative of Gen. Zebulon Montgomery Pike, for whom Pikes Peak is named, Anson Rudd had his own adventurous spirit when he and his wife, Harriet, set out for California. When Harriet saw the beautiful climate and bountiful game on August 7, 1860, she decided that Cañon City was where she wanted to stay. Anson Spencer Rudd (standing), born to Anson and Harriett, is said to be the first white child born in Cañon City to grow into adulthood. Anson Rudd Sr. loved poetry and wrote verses about many of the events in the early history of Cañon City. The Rudds built their stone home in 1881 next to their cabin, where it still rests at the Royal Gorge Regional Museum and History Center. Anson Rudd became the first territorial prison warden.

TO ARMS! TO ARMS!

A meeting of the citizens of Canon City will be held at

MURRAY'S HALL,

AT 2 P. M., TO-DAY, OCTOBER 8, 1879,

For the Purpose of organizing for protection against the Indians now within our borders.

Record Print, Cañon City

Murray Billiard Hall and Saloon had a public hall on the second floor at 305 Main Street, where several early churches began. An uprising in another county prompted this notice, but the Ute Indians, including respected Chief Ouray and his wife, Chipeta, wintered in the Cañon City area for years without much trouble for the settlers. Mrs. B. F. Rockafellow told of Native American women with their noses flattened against the windows, begging for her delicious biscuits.

James Lewis Harrison (right) and John Henry Harrison (left), shown with their sister Mary Virginia Macon, wife of Thomas Macon, moved to Cañon City in a covered wagon with their widowed mother, Ann, in September 1864 as part of the "Resurrectionist" movement after the Civil War. John partnered with Thomas, bringing new leadership and culture to Cañon City. Together they opened a mercantile in Cañon City, and Thomas also began farming, improving the area with irrigation ventures, such as the Cañon City Hydraulic and Irrigating Ditch Company. John held various posts, such as county commissioner, county treasurer, and mayor, where his support helped build the first county courthouse.

The beautiful Harrison-Hawthorne home at 901 River Street caused quite a stir when the first lawn in town, consisting of clover and oats, was installed. John was a leading fruit grower with at least three orchards in East Cañon City, and he built the Harrison Block at 609–615 Main Street.

This Henry Mack lumberyard photograph was taken in 1875 at the corner of Sixth and Main Streets. Merchants sold supplies shipped on wagons and later the Grape Creek Narrow Gauge to towns, including Rosita, Querida, and Silver Cliff. Much of the lumber used to build the Daily Record building and many other downtown structures came from Mack's lumberyard.

This lumber wagon train pulled by oxen is ready to make a delivery, possibly to Cripple Creek and Victor after fires in 1896 and 1899 leveled those towns. The buildings in the background include the First Methodist Church at Fifth and Main Streets.

David Erwin Gibson, born in Waverly, Illinois, owned more than 16 lumberyards in several states. The Gibson lumberyard at Eighth and River Streets was later sold to the Short family. Gibson built his fortune after the Cripple Creek fire in 1896 destroyed most of the town and more, so when Victor suffered the same fate in 1899, Gibson choose to build with stone.

After a successful Civil War career, Capt. B. F. Rockafellow moved to Colorado as a miner and later settled in Cañon City. He became one of the most prolific real estate developers in the area and was postmaster for 10 years. Rockafellow, related to the New York Rockefellers, owned Fruitmere orchard, one of the largest in the area, and shipped fruit all over the country as far away as Chicago. He made as much as $45,000 with his fruit business in 1901.

The Rockafellow home at 121 Main Street was thought to be a bit pretentious for the neighborhood when it was built but was constructed with 18-inch-thick adobe walls to keep it warm in the winter and cool in the summer. When the Cañon City Arbor and Floricultural Society formed to beautify the town, Rockafellow and his father, George, helped plant over 1,500 trees and shrubs, and some are shown here with protective coverings. The home was razed in the early 1950s after the chimney was blown over in a windstorm and crashed down to the first floor.

The stage stop in Cañon City was located on the southwest corner of Seventh and Main Streets. A trip on the narrow Shelf Road took six hours from Cañon City to Cripple Creek and four hours for the return trip at the cost of $3 in 1892. Teams were changed several times, with 36 horses used daily. There was only enough room for one team to go through at a time, so the lead horses had a bell on them to warn oncoming teams, whereas the team going down the trail had to stop and back to a wider spot in the road to let the other pass.

Cañon City was once a transportation hub to Leadville, Rosita, Silver Cliff, Cripple Creek, Colorado Springs, and other areas. Stage rules for travel written by David A. Butterfield and cited in an early *Cañon City Daily Record* article included, "Do not grease your hair with bear grease or buffalo tallow before boarding the stage. Do not point out places where Indian attacks took place. If you must drink pass the bottle around after all it is polite to share. If the stage is attacked, do not jump off; you might get hurt by the jump but you WILL get hurt by the Indians!"

When Frederick A. Raynolds opened the Raynolds Bank in 1874 in the lobby of the Strathmore Hotel, he was the youngest bank president in the state. At age 30, Raynolds was mentioned in the *History of the Arkansas Valley Colorado*, dated 1881, as the most prominent bank president in the state. He went on to open at least six more banks in Colorado.

Built in 1879 at Fourth and Main Streets and called "the Ornament of Cañon City," Raynolds Bank was constructed in the Gothic Revival style of pink-hued stone hauled from Castle Rock. The foundation limestone was quarried at the nearby penitentiary, with the original cost to build estimated to be $25,000. After many years in service, the Raynolds Bank was recently restored to its original beauty.

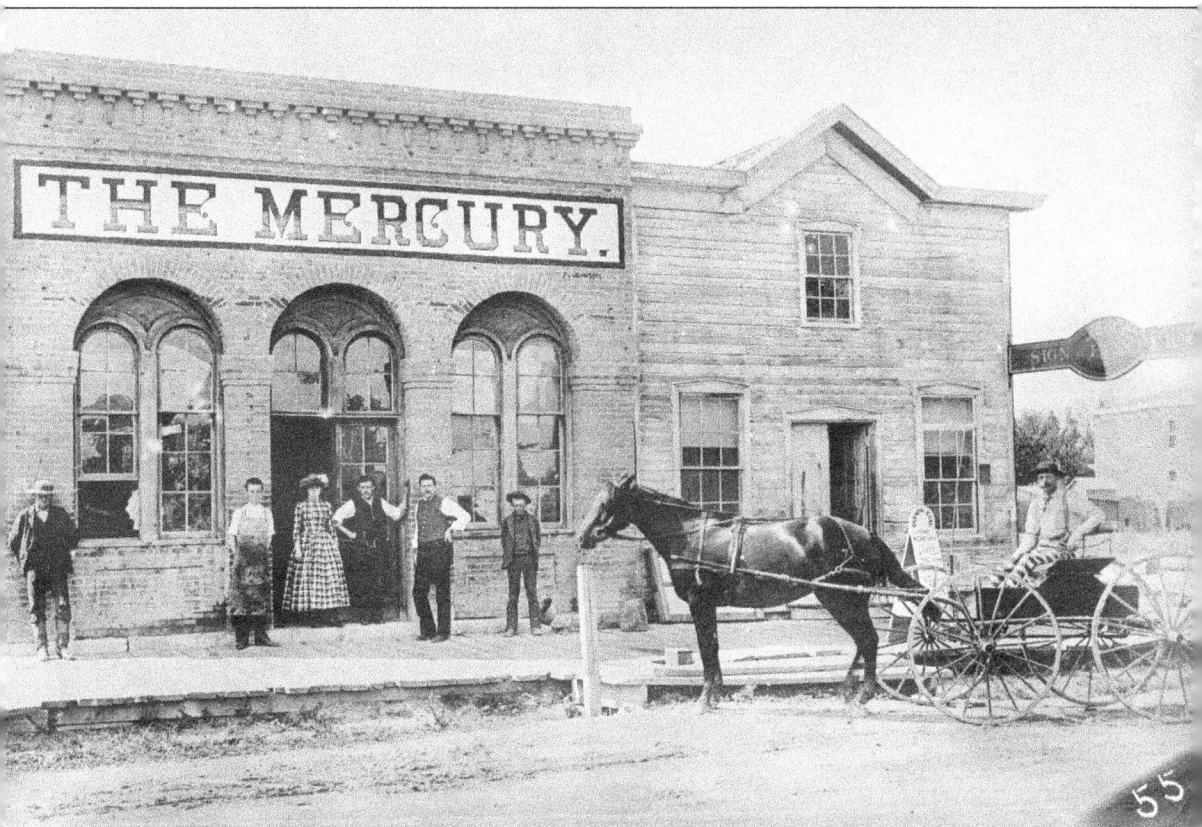

Over 20 newspapers have kept Cañon City up to date since it was founded. The *Mercury* was one of three newspapers serving Cañon City from 1884 to 1885. Operating at Fifth and Main Streets, the editor and staff are shown standing proudly in front of the building. The *Mercury* was known for its political views that ran to the Republican Party and also for its up-to-date news of the region, having several area correspondents retained. This photograph shows an inmate waiting in a carriage. Inmates provided many services to the wardens and their families, including driving them around town.

Built in 1881 when Colorado had only been a state for five years and Cañon City an incorporated city for nine years, the Fremont County Courthouse was located on Macon Street near First Street and was believed to be the oldest in the state. The photograph also shows a stone building located on Greenwood Avenue that housed the county jail. A beautiful building for the time, it was in such dire disrepair due to poor foundation conditions that in 1886 the entire building was disassembled and rebuilt, using the same materials on better soil at Fourth and Macon Streets. There it served the public until a new building was constructed in 1961 and was torn down in 1965. In 1935, a 500-pound clock weight snapped loose as it was being wound from its cable and crashed through the ceiling and into the district courtroom. Court was not in session at the time.

The Cañon City coronet band is shown practicing for a parade at Fifth and Main Streets in the mid-1880s. In the background are the First Methodist Church, erected in 1878, the first public library, and the building that housed the *Mercury* newspaper. Originally called the Handy and McGee, the building on the right was later renamed the Sulphide building after Lyman Robison remodeled it and it housed the city's largest general store. These buildings stood at this location until Robison constructed the Annex Hall and R. L. Smith erected his dry goods store.

The Annex Hall was one of three buildings Lyman Robison constructed on Main Street. Built in 1903, it was where the Ray Haws band entertained dancers for many years. To finance his three businesses in the downtown area, Robison used money from his Leadville mines. Designed by C. C. Rittenhouse, with ideas inspired by a trip to Europe, and by Robison and his wife, the Annex was the finest and most expensive building in town at that time. Robison also added the Apex and Sulphide buildings, which were named after his mines.

The stately mansion built at 12 Riverside Street by Robison for a cost of $20,000 in 1884 was designed by G. W. Roe and featured a two-story kitchen. Robison made his fortune in mining interests in Leadville, but this is where the Robison family lived to escape the harsh Leadville winters. The Robison mansion was the site of many parties, and the family held a beloved place in the hearts of the city residents.

The Maupin family resided where the Cañon City Public Library Park at the corner of Fifth and Macon Streets is now. Gen. Joseph Maupin was known for his involvement in Colorado politics and for his many contributions to the area, including contracting the post office and the Maupin buildings, located on opposing corners of Fifth and Macon Streets. He came to Cañon City in 1884, and in 1890 at age 36, he became the Colorado state attorney general. Well liked by all who knew him, he made an unsuccessful run for governor but had a law practice for many years. Maupin and his wife, the former Lilly McClure, held parties and informal gatherings at their home and were known for their hospitality.

Two

THE FRUITED PLAIN

After the first apple orchard in the county and likely the state of Colorado was started by Jesse Frazer in 1867 in Florence just east of Cañon City, the fruit industry in the area caught on like wildfire. Hundreds of orchards sprang up, and soon Cañon City was supplying fruit, such as apples, pears, plums, cherries, and many other varieties for the entire region.

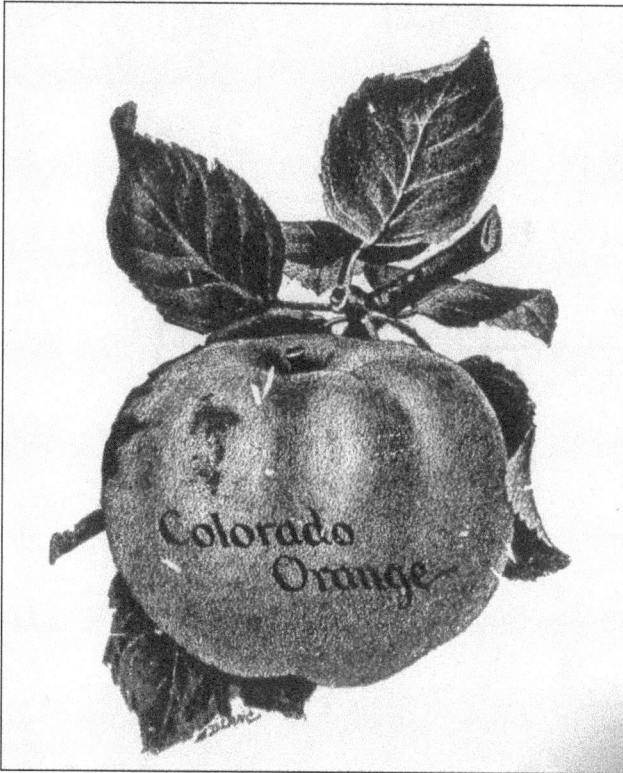

The names of several apple varieties have not survived through the years, but some interesting kinds included Gano, Colorado Orange, and Arkansas black. Cañon City fruit were renowned nationwide and won over 27 medals at the 1904 Louisiana Purchase Exposition at the world's fair's Palace of Agriculture.

B. F. Rockafellow is seen in his carriage and Phil Sheridan is driving the wagon loaded with fruit for market. Most orchards were small fruit farms ranging from two to ten acres. Cañon City yielded enormous amounts of fruit due in large part to the profuse irrigation canal network over the city and county, with apples being the largest fruit crop and strawberries the next. Frequently limbs needed to be held up with stakes in order to keep the trees from breaking under the weight of the heavy apples. Fruit was sold all over the Rocky Mountain region, where it was welcomed in the rich mining towns of Cripple Creek, Victor, Fairplay, Leadville, and many others.

FRUIT
DOM...
IN AWAY
AN ON CITY COLO
PPLE DAY
EPT. 20. 1894

The Music and Blossom Festival is held each year during the first weekend in May. Originally it began as Fruit Day, a fall celebration held in September when the railroads ran excursion trains from Denver and Colorado Springs in order to promote the fruit industry. Livery stables were pressed to provide rigs to take people on tours of the orchards, and over 36,000 pounds of produce was given away to celebrants on September 20, 1894.

Cañon City's premier spring celebration has a fine parade each year and is host to marching bands from around the region. It went through several name changes before finally settling on Cañon City Music and Blossom Festival. During the peak of the orchard years, Cañon City was unsurpassed in spring flower glory and became an annual destination for sightseers from all over America.

The Cañon City Music and Blossom Festival has crowned many beauties through the years. High school girls have competed in the Blossom Pageant and have ridden in music and blossom parades for decades. The crowning of the blossom queen has been a significant honor for the young ladies through the years and continues today.

In an early Fruit Day parade on September 15, 1896, with A. H. Davis as the grand marshal and a committee of town notables, including T. M. Hardy, Frederick A. Raynolds, Dallas "Dall" DeWeese, N. F. Handy, and J. H. Peabody. All of the fire departments made a showing, as did uniformed bands, including a Napoleon gun drill commanded by Capt. R. S. Kincaid. At noon, the long-awaited big event was the free distribution of thousands of pounds of the most delicious fruit to the community and visitors. This later flap jack race photograph shows that everyone gets involved in the merriment of the festival.

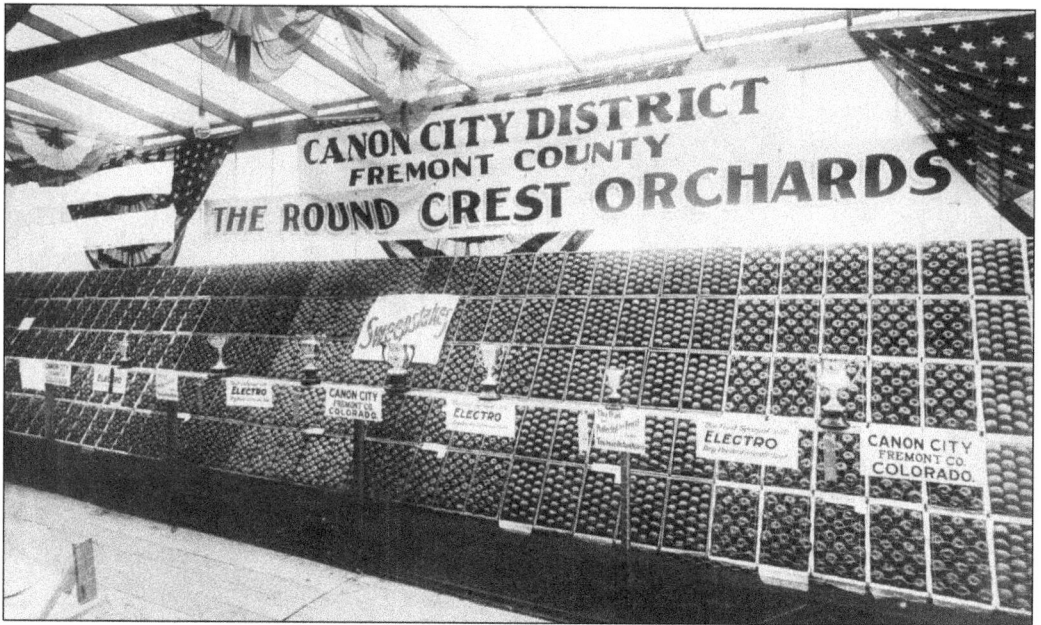

At the American Apple Congress in Denver in 1911, Cañon City apples won an impressive eight silver cups. The exhibit was packed and shown by Phil Sheridan, who worked for B. F. Rockafellow. Later in December of that year, fruit growers from all over the state of Colorado visited Cañon City for evaluations of Fremont county apples, a tour, and to discuss growing procedures and practices to further the growth of the industry in the state.

Land that was once dry and arid became fertile farmland through an aggressive irrigation canal installation. A labyrinth of irrigation canals and ditches cross the farmland in Cañon City, and many innovative, pioneering irrigation practices turned the area into a lush, green farming community and highlighted the development of the region.

Completed in 1904, the DeWeese Reservoir was built to provide irrigation to the newly developed Lincoln Park and South Cañon developments. Land was sold as orchard and farmland. As he began to lose patrons in his developing real estate ventures due to insufficient water supplies, Dallas "Dall" DeWeese made good on his claim: "These people should have a good and permanent water supply; the mountain will supply it; I will find it." Built on Grape Creek in the Wet Mountain Valley, the large dam was built of cut stone and 35 carloads of cement.

Cañon City celery was regarded as the finest grown in the state. Considered a delicacy on American tables during the winter holidays, it brought top prices. During the first part of the 20th century, there were many celery farms along Canal Street (now Tunnel Drive) in the Hot Springs addition and in Lincoln Park.

Many ranchers turned to growing potatoes to supplement slow cattle seasons. The mountains and cattle ranges north of Cañon City are dotted with now-unused potato farms and potato cellars.

Several canneries were needed due to the large fruit and vegetable harvests, with the first one being the Colorado Cannery Company, located at Eighth and Water Streets. Jones Brothers, a nationwide distributor of canned goods, also did a large business in the same location with a satellite plant.

Brightly colored labels were found on the cans produced in Cañon City, such as this one from the Round Crest Canning Company. The label shown features a bright red background with contrasting lettering and a bright orange pumpkin. The label also shows a painting of the Royal

ROYAL GORGE

REGISTERED U.S PATENT OFFICE

PACKED BY
THE ROUND CREST CANNING CO.
CANON CITY, COLO.

Gorge Canyon before the Royal Gorge Bridge was built. In the lower part of the painting, the hanging bridge over the Arkansas River can be seen.

J. M. Fickus built the first gristmill near First and Main Streets in 1868. It was a buhr mill of small capacity that was enlarged and improved through the years, and it burned more than once, causing quite a stir in the community. The mill went through several owners, and when it was reconstructed in 1884, it was contracted to produce 200 sacks of flour per day. Many reputed it to be the best constructed and most complete flour mill in the state.

These men are spraying for leaf-roller insects that could attack the apple tree leaves and destroy entire orchards. The sprayer shown is the first powered sprayer in Cañon City and was owned by the Kissinger farm around 1910.

Two men and a child stand by their asparagus pick of the day from a farm on Twelfth Street and Grand Avenue. Notice the repair on the solid rear tire. Wild asparagus grows along many irrigation ditches in the city and surrounding area, making the annual spring asparagus growing season something of a secret-keeping competition.

Until the 1920s, the high school was closed so the students could help with orchard and farm harvests during part of the autumn. The John Deere Model L tractor with the young man driving is pulling a sled behind, helping to cut the corners of the cornfield.

The Cañon City area has been home to many dairies from small, single-cow backyards to large commercial producers. This little boy was learning to milk in the dairy housed at the Independent Order of Odd Fellows orphanage on Fifteenth Street.

Dairies played a significant part in the settling of Cañon City, as shown in this photograph of the Golden Rule Dairy. Milk from Cañon City is well known for its smooth, creamy taste and high nutritional content. Most of the dairies in the area have been family-run businesses, but the prison has also run a large dairy herd for decades.

Three

RANCHES, RODEOS, AND COUNTY FAIRS

Wharton (Whart) Pigg, prominent rancher, friend of famous big-game hunter Dallas (Dall) DeWeese, and contemporary of Theodore Roosevelt, all men with conservation in mind, established a private game preserve at his Stirrup Ranch. Well versed in the fauna of the West, his intent was to save deer, elk, bear, and other game animals from extinction by breeding specimens for eastern zoos and private collections. This photograph shows a 1902 delivery of 40 elk from Jackson Hole, Wyoming, to the Stirrup Ranch just below Black Mountain.

On May 5, 1904, after hundreds of attempts to take down the notorious grizzly bear "Old Mose," who had killed Jacob Radcliff in 1883 and terrorized hundreds of cattle, horses, and settlers in the county for over 20 years, W. J. Anthony, accompanied by rancher Wharton (Whart) Pigg, finally killed him with the help of Anthony's tracking dogs. "Old Mose" was brought to Cañon City, where he was placed on display at Wright and Morgan's butcher shop and his meat was cut up and made into bear steaks and sold to the community.

This photograph of a cattle roundup at the Witcher Ranch in 1910 shows both cowboys and probably a Ford Model T. Many ranchers had vehicles at this time, usually sturdy Studebakers or Buicks. Gravity-fed carburetors made travel up hills frustrating, as they occasionally had to be backed up the hill.

Ranchers from around the area show up to help each other with branding each year. Usually there was plenty of grass, water, and good climate for Cañon City–area ranches to produce large herds and prosperous families, but the area has known some hard droughts and large, fast-moving storms throughout the years when beef ranchers did not fare well. This photograph shows branding time at the Beckham Ranch in 1897.

Cowboys are rounding up and catching workhorses at the Wilson Creek camp. Most cow horses were compact, range-raised animals weighing between 800 and 1,000 pounds. Horses ran on the open range and rarely went far from their birthplaces. Tol Witcher was known to have some of the meanest, hard-riding horses in the area, even supplying stock to the first rodeos in Cripple Creek. One of his horses, Tornado, became a famous bucking horse and was said in a September 22, 1910, newspaper article to be "a veritable demon in horseflesh."

Area ranchers and cowboys enjoy their meal while rounding up cattle on Wilson Creek north of Cañon City. In the photograph are, from left to right, John Vivian, Frank Taylor (camp cook), Glenn Brown, Wharton (Whart) Pigg, Levi Haley, Taliaferro "Tol" Witcher, Billy Farrell, and Billy Witherspoon. In a letter to his brother George, Brown stated, "Cattle are at a good price and ready sale and I will sell my yearling steers as long as I can get twenty dollars or more for them."

There are two chuck wagons in this picture. Frequently one wagon was outfitted with cooking necessities and the other carried bedrolls, personal items, and extra supplies. Famed rancher Charles Goodnight is credited with creating the first chuck wagon for a cattle drive from Texas to Denver, where it passed through the area and land holdings he owned close to the Hardscrabble area between Cañon City and Pueblo. On one such drive, one of Goodnight's cowboys recalled a minor argument when some Cañon City farmers tried to stop the cattle drive from crossing the Arkansas River. The cowboys on the large cattle drives and settlers frequently were at odds because settlers resented cowboys driving the herds through their farmlands.

Cow camps were stocked for the roundup and cowboys were well supplied with coffee, steak, fried potatoes, dried fruit, and hot sourdough biscuits. Early entertainment for the cowboys included chuck wagon races at local celebrations. Each three-man team raced around a track, unharnessed the team, pitched a tent, and started a fire in the sheet-iron stove. Because the cowboy teams came from around the state, they camped at the fairgrounds after the competitions, using the gear they brought with them for the race.

Southern Colorado around Cañon City is known for its mild climate and good range for cattle, but occasionally deep snows make it quite a challenge. In this photograph, the rancher, probably on the Hatchet Ranch, is driving horses through the deep snow to make a trail for the cattle to get to food and water.

Adorned with a fine law library and built with hand-cut stone, the home of the Murray family also was outfitted with a two-story barn that even had a fine slate billiard table. The family planted a large apple orchard and extensive alfalfa fields. A cozy, well-appointed boardinghouse for railroad crews was tended by the Murray family for a time. Embers from a passing steam locomotive caught the barn on fire and destroyed it.

Ranch wives were a hardy bunch and were expected to feed many from family and ranch hands to occasional guests. The Cañon City area was plentiful in wild fruits, such as chokecherries, wild plums, rosehips, and wild raspberries. Gardens were easy to grow in the lower elevations, and the women enjoyed the company of other ranching wives during canning and butchering seasons. Women worked hard, doing whatever was needed to keep the ranch house in order inside and out. It was their duty to see that the children were given training in everyday ranching duties, as well as oversee any education, social activities, and cultural training.

Well dressed and ready for a ride, Henrietta Witcher sits sidesaddle on her horse in 1895. In the waning years of the 19th century, women were moving to the city in larger numbers than men because there were many more women than men in rural areas. When they moved to the city, it was the young working girls who were spending substantial sums on clothes, makeup, and amusements. Ranch life afforded young women few opportunities for personal wealth and interest.

Originally named the Old Settler's Reunion, Cañon City Wild West Days were an example of early rodeo competitions. In a 1913 *Cañon City Record* article, a listing of events included bucking contests, rough riding, wild horse races, mess wagon races, wild steer races, a fancy ropewalk, and roping contests. The event was put on entirely by the cattlemen of the area, and the executive committee included notable ranchers, such as E. C. Higgins, Charles Canterbury, Dudley P. Van Buskirk, and Will A. McKenzie. In this photograph, the cowboy holding the horse is biting the animal's ear to keep him steady during a wild horse race.

"This is what is left of Snake the outlaw's first try at running away with a rider in 1903," stated Van Buskirk. "When we opened the gate Snake started to back out and run for the ridges, then he hit a bog hole and went down." The cowboy was able to get the horse to stay down long enough to save his saddle.

Shown in this photograph are Robert Nelson (left) and Charlie Canterbury, who were in charge of the stock for the Top O' the World Rodeo in Victor, one of the first rodeos in the country. The bronc Bad Whiskey is doing his best to unseat his rider. Charlie Chess won the grand prize for his ride that day and was presented a saddle and bridle outfit complete with gold spurs valued at $500.

Here in 1940, the Beef Club exhibits prime animals in the 600 block of Main Street in front of the Palace Drug Store. Several men stand by to judge the stock, as well as purchase the beef from the exhibitors. Fremont County 4-H competitors have sold livestock at the county fair to help pay for college for decades, making the annual sale a highlight of their year.

Some young Poultry Club exhibitors are shown in 1944, finishing their year with a judging contest in front of the Fremont Bank at Sixth and Main Streets. In March of that year, 50 boys and girls were each given 50 chicks from the Pennington Hatchery in order to raise and learn about poultry farming. Each showman brought the four best chickens in their flock to try to win a $25 war bond.

Built in 1922 primarily for military purposes, the National Guard Armory housed flower and livestock shows for the county for several years. High school basketball games and dances for various clubs were held there, as well as several Ku Klux Klan events and concerts—with the Rolling Stones playing there early in their career. Shown in this photograph are several chickens in cages draped with festive bunting. Various 4-H exhibits also line the walls.

Four

PLACES OF
SPECIAL INTEREST

The Garden Park
Fossil Area just north
of Cañon City has
long been known
as one of the first
dinosaur discovery sites
in the country and is
designated a national
natural landmark. The
Colorado state fossil is
a stegosaurus excavated
in 1937 by local
high school teacher
F. C. "Prof." Kessler
and his students.

Prof. Othneil Marsh of Yale College and Prof. E. D. Cope of the Academy of Natural Sciences in Philadelphia, both highly ambitious and wishing to earn a high standing in the young and exciting science of paleontology, waged a highly publicized and bitter rivalry, with each accusing the other of theft, spying, and invasion of each other's digs. It ultimately led to confusion in identification of their specimens that took years and many other scientists to sort out. This photograph of the fossil bones of the camarasaurus supremus was taken by C. W. Talbot for O. W. Lucas.

Cañon City adventurer and famous big-game hunter Dallas (Dall) Deweese found another pastime when his interest in hunting for fossils turned to success at the discovery of a brontosaurus diplodocus, which became the first dinosaur in the Denver Museum of Natural History (now the Denver Museum of Nature and Science). In addition, Garden Park area specimens are housed in the Smithsonian, Cleveland Museum of Natural History, American Museum of Natural History in New York City, Carnegie Museum in Pittsburgh, and many other museums nationwide.

Discovered in 1876 in the Garden Park area by M. P. Felch and his family, the stegosaurus stenops shown in the Smithsonian Institution in Washington, D.C., was one of many dinosaurs excavated by O. C. Marsh and his contemporaries and displayed worldwide. For decades, there was an argument as to how the plates on the stegosaurus's tail should be positioned, either staggered or in pairs, and both versions are shown in displays and publications.

"Oil Spring," the second-oldest oil seep in the nation, was discovered in 1862 just east of Four Mile Creek in the Garden Park area (formerly known as Oil Creek). The first oil well, the Drake Well, was found in 1859 in Titusville, Pennsylvania. The discovery of oil seeping from the Jurassic Morrison foundation led to the discovery of the first large oil field, the Florence Pool, 7 miles south. It put Colorado on the map as a large oil producer.

Oil production became a huge business in the Cañon City vicinity, with many wells producing black gold, such as the one shown in this Chandler Petroleum Company photograph. There are several men and women shown with their vehicles proudly standing in front of the oil well and buildings.

Consumed by Ute Indians for many years for healthful benefits, Cañon City residents and tourists alike enjoyed the Soda Springs. The Iron Duke and the Little Ute, side-by-side springs, were thought to provide relief of liver and kidney ailments and thought of as an aid for digestion. City fathers took great care of the springs and built many improvements there. Early pioneers settled around the Soda Springs, and the town grew outward from that point, with places of interest, such as the Four Mile area and Eight Mile Hill measured from the Soda Springs.

During an expansion of U.S. Highway 50 in 1949, Soda Point was paved over much to the dismay of Cañon City residents who tried to bring it back into operation. It was too late, and only a small trickle was able to be found.

Native American legends, including a romantic duel for the hand of a fair maiden between Ute and Blackfeet Indian warriors abound regarding the Temple Canyon area. The site is also said to be where a battle raged between the Ute tribes and U.S. soldiers. The canyon has a natural theater at least 30 feet deep and 70 feet wide. A vigorous hike crossing Grape Creek from the surrounding picnic areas was well visited by adventurous Cañon City residents and tourists alike.

Built with convict labor under the direction of Warden John Cleghorn and overseer John Allen, construction on Skyline Drive was started in 1904. D. E. Gibson was instrumental in raising the private funds necessary from citizens of Cañon City for blasting powder to build it. This beautiful drive was to show Cañon City and the surrounding country in the best possible way and to provide an interesting pleasure trip for visitors to the city. The name Skyline Boulevard was the original deeded name but was known as Skyline Drive early on. Automobile and carriage drivers argued both in and out of court for several years about who had the right of way, as it was deemed by several near-miss incidents that both did not fit safely on the drive together. Skyline Drive gave adventurous visitors an exciting thrill when looking over the growing city. (Courtesy Library of Congress.)

The first known homesteader to the beautiful Red Canyon Park area north of Cañon City, Otto Morganstein was apparently friendly with Ute Indian Chief Colorow, who was said by others to be a pretty mean character, especially when fortified with liquor. Whenever one of Morganstein's horses wandered off, Colorow sent a brave out to retrieve the wayward animal.

Granted to Cañon City as a city park on March 2, 1923, at the request of resident and congressman Guy Hardy, the 640-acre Red Canyon Park features beautiful natural red rock formations and grand monoliths of stone. The roads through the park were built with volunteers from Cañon City. The park was dedicated on Decoration Day, May 30, 1924, in an elaborate ceremony with hundreds of visitors in the new park.

Ernest Sell originally created Sells Lake on his homestead in order to supply ice to Cañon City residents, then at considerable expense to himself, he created Sell's Island resort for the recreation of Cañon City residents and tourists. The resort, located south of the Arkansas River just under Pump Hill, was elaborately planted with a variety of flowers and trees. A dance floor was erected at the edge of the lake, and orchestras entertained local couples through the summer months. Boats were available for rent, and the lake was popular for ice-skating in the winter.

The St. Cloud Hotel was built in 1883 in Silver Cliff in the waning years of the Colorado silver boom. It was dismantled and moved by wagon to Cañon City in 1886, where it enjoyed a long and prosperous history as one of the grandest hotels of the city. Notables visiting the St. Cloud included Buffalo Bill, actors with the Colorado Moving Picture Company, Tom Mix, Burt Lancaster, Slim Pickens, Broderick Crawford, and Charles Bronson. They all enjoyed a comfortable and gracious stay.

With a temperature of 104 degrees, the mineral water was thought to have healing properties. Dr. J. L Prentiss built a 38-room, three-story hotel and health spa 1 mile west of town at the entrance to the Royal Gorge Canyon in 1873. Early railroad customers from Cripple Creek, Victor, Leadville, and other surrounding mining towns walked across the footbridge to reach the hotel and the bathhouse or took a hack ride from town. During the late 1890s, the hotel was a popular Cañon City social center for dinners, dances, and high school–sponsored parties.

The McClure House Hotel at 331 Main Street was opened by W. H. McClure on October 4, 1874, with a huge glittering gala where Mayor Thomas Macon spoke and Cañon City pioneer Anson Rudd shared a poem specially written for the occasion. An underground mall of sorts with four shops was in use before the 1900s, as evidenced by amethyst-colored skylights in the sidewalk on Main Street. The hotel shared quarters with the Fremont County Bank, the first bank in Cañon City before Frederick A. Raynolds built his impressive Raynolds Bank across the street.

Remodeled, modernized, and given a thorough facelift, the McClure House Hotel was renamed the Strathmore in memory of a Scottish estate visited by new owners C. R. C. Dye and his wife in 1900. When it reopened on January 31, 1901, over 200 Cañon City guests arrived to view the grand hotel and were treated to a nine-course meal where the tables were beautifully set with ferns and carnations. Elegant meals were the norm at the Strathmore and included such delights as roast wild mallard duck with currant jelly, English plum pudding, and dairy products from the hotel's own herd of Jersey cows.

Located at 302 South Ninth Street, the Rio Grand Hotel opened in 1907, at which time a gathering of over 1,000 people braved the rain to visit and inspect the modern, new hotel. Because of its close proximity to the D&RG (Denver and Rio Grande) railroad depot directly across the street, the hotel was the site where several presidents and presidential candidates stopped to make their speeches. This 1952 photograph shows Pres. Harry Truman making a speech to a crowd from the back of his train when the building was named the Ott Hotel.

Where the mighty Royal Gorge Canyon of the Arkansas River is at its most narrow point, an engineering marvel would need to take place in order for trains to get through to the mining towns. The gorge was over 1,000 feet deep at that point and only 30 feet wide. Blasting huge amounts of rock was impossible to set a rail on, so another solution was needed. The 274-foot hanging bridge was to be set from two trusses by cables, with a girder to carry the track. Completed at a cost of $12,000 by May 1879, the narrow gauge was laid, and on May 7, 1879, the first passenger train passed over the bridge and went to the end of the track near Parkdale.

64

The half-mile-deep Royal Gorge Canyon has attracted brave sightseers for many years, as shown in this photograph of several women standing at an early observation point with one seated by her dog. The raging Arkansas River is shown at the bottom of the great canyon. In May 1906, a total of 5,000 acres of land was deeded to Cañon City by Congress for use as a municipal park, where a stone observation pavilion and ultimately the Royal Gorge Bridge and Park were later built.

In 1929, the Royal Gorge Bridge, the world's highest suspension bridge, was built as a tourist attraction. Like the man shown high atop the tower, most of the 80 men who worked on the 1,260-foot bridge were from Cañon City and had little or no prior experience in construction. They were paid about 35¢ an hour, and despite their lack in experience, they built the bridge. Work started June 5 was finished in six months with virtually no injuries and or deaths at a cost of $350,000.

December 8, 1929, was a banner day for the large, enthusiastic crowd of residents, sightseers, and dignitaries that made the journey to the opening of the Royal Gorge Bridge for promoter Lon Piper and engineer George C. Cole. Cañon City mayor T. Lee Witcher was in the first car to drive across the span. Speeches, bands, and even a wedding marked the big event.

As shown in this early postcard, the Royal Gorge Bridge is an impressive sight. For over 80 years, it has been attracting thousands of sightseers from all over the world. The park features several attractions, including the world's steepest incline railway reaching down to the bottom of the gorge, an aerial tramway, and a sky-coaster.

Five

RELIGION, EDUCATION, AND SOCIAL GROUPS

Early schools in the Cañon City area were taught at the home of the teacher, and in more rural settings, the teacher stayed at the home of a local family. Perhaps because of the territorial prison, a favorite game at the Garden Park School was "guards and convicts," in which the children were divided up and the "convicts" scattered into the field to be caught by the "guards."

School Dist. No. 4, Cañon City, Col.

Country schools such as the District Four School, also called the Fruitmere School, in the lower Four-Mile area in East Cañon City, were the center of the community. Teachers were expected by the school board to "endeavor on all proper occasions to impress on the minds of their pupils the principles of morality and virtue and sacred regard for truth, neatness, order, sobriety, industry and frugality."

Washington School, - Between 6th - 7th St. Mason ave. where the present Court House now stands.

Built 1880   Razed 1960

On October 6, 1880, a three-year high school was started with a weekly tuition cost of 75¢ per student. Course offerings at the Washington School included algebra, bookkeeping, rhetoric, physiology, botany, geology, zoology, geography, and philosophy. One rule of the new school was that anyone wearing a gun to school would be subject to expulsion. The bell tower was a magnet for childish pranks. In 1901 or 1902, several boys wrangled a cow up into the bell tower, where it resided overnight.

Considered one of the most modern schools at the time of its construction in 1894 at the corner of Fourteenth and Main Streets, the Lincoln School was attended by many of Cañon City's children for over three generations. One student of note was famous Detroit Lions all-pro football player Jack Christiansen, raised at Cañon City's Independent Order of Odd Fellows orphanage. He started his highly successful football career while attending the Lincoln School.

Roosevelt High School, built at the corner of Ninth Street and College Avenue in 1901, was Cañon City's first high school building and boasted two bowling alleys in the basement for girls, showering facilities for athletes, an armory for the cadets, and two outdoor tennis courts. The auditorium was used for public concerts, lectures, and community gatherings. The last class to graduate from this building was in 1925.

When dedicated on October 23, 1925, the modern, new Cañon City High School building was referred to by Mary Bradford, Colorado state superintendent of public instruction, as a "temple of learning" and "a laboratory for the making of good citizenship." The school was built with funds from a large bond greatly supported by the community.

Reportedly this is Cañon City High School's first girls' basketball team. The students chose the tiger as their mascot in 1920. The school colors started out gold and silver, but in the fall of 1920, the students voted to make the colors black and gold, which remain today.

Cañon City is proud of the history of the Junior ROTC program, which is among the oldest and most successful in the nation. It was a mandatory course for sophomore boys until 1974, when it became an elective. Girls have also been active with their own Kadette Corps, which were then integrated into the full program. During the deadly prison riot on October 3, 1929, several of the ROTC cadets were pressed into service, and the .30-caliber model 1903 Springfield rifles they used in training were also loaned to men in town for riot service.

Located in the 600 block of Pike Avenue, the Colorado Collegiate and Military Institute was built in 1881 as a prep and military school for boys. Because of constant financial troubles from the start, the academy opened its doors to girls in 1883. Cost for the 40-week school session was $300, which included tuition, room and board, and use of rifles. The military academy never overcame its financial woes and was closed in 1886.

The original building for the St. Scholastica Academy became the location of the military academy and opened as a girls' school in 1890 under the name of Mount St. Scholastica Academy. Townspeople were initially suspicious of the Benedictine nuns and did not want them to shop in their businesses when they arrived. A wayward milk cow eased their distress by providing needed nourishment until a parishioner introduced them to shopkeepers, guaranteeing their credit and making it so they were able to shop freely. The school was open for 111 years and became a proud addition to the community.

Organized on January 23, 1867, the Cumberland Presbyterian Church was the oldest congregation of this denomination in Colorado. Later the congregation built a church on land donated by Cañon City resident and then governor Anson Rudd. In 1908, the Cumberland Presbyterian Church joined the Presbyterians to create the United Presbyterian Church, and the building was torn down.

The Presbyterian church was organized with 10 members—one man and nine women. As they outgrew their small building, it was determined that a larger church was needed. S. Ward was the general contractor when ground was broken in August 1900. The cornerstone was laid in December of that same year. Built in a Richardson Romanesque style complete with a Queen Anne–style bell tower, the church is constructed of reddish- or buff-colored rough-cut stone.

The Abbey School started in 1926 was conducted by the Benedictine fathers. Its Tudor Gothic–style building was ranked among the finest structures in the state. There were three parts to the building, including a chapel, refectory, and the monastery. The school was started in the main building, and later a large school and gymnasium were added. It was a boarding school, but many of the young men in town were enrolled there also. The team mascot was a bear, and the school newspaper was titled the *Growler*.

In May 1864, Baptists from Appanoose County, Iowa, headed to Colorado in covered wagons and settled in young Cañon City. Built in 1869 in the 400 block of Main Street, the little church was made of adobe bricks and had two rooms and a baptistery under the pulpit. The church prospered under the leadership of the first pastor, Rev. B. M. Adams, until the grand First Baptist Church building was constructed at Seventh and Macon Streets in 1892.

A modern First Baptist Church was erected in 1892, constructed of red sandstone hauled by James Higdon from Harding Brothers Quarry from the base of Fremont Peak. Stone for many Cañon City buildings was also taken from there. Architect D. A. Bradbury was in charge of the project and also was the creative thought behind several other early Cañon City buildings. The tower on the left was removed in the early 1950s.

Built in 1879, the First Methodist Church on the northeast corner of Main and Fifth Streets cost the congregation $4,500 to construct and was a prominent building in early Cañon City history. Rev. George Murray organized the First Methodist Church and came to Colorado from Chicago in 1865 accompanied by armed men hired to keep him and his wife safe from Native American attacks. Attention was called to the church meetings by "a negro walking up and down the street in front of the building ringing a dinner bell."

Originally constructed in 1899 and later enlarged in 1906, the Methodist Episcopal church, located at Eighth and Main Streets, was dedicated with an elaborate ceremony. At the ceremony, a small copper box containing scriptures; the Methodist discipline and hymnal; membership lists; copies of the *Cañon City Clipper*, *Cañon City Record*, and *Cañon City Times* newspapers; the architect's card; and a historical sketch of the church were fitted into the aperture made for it in the southwest corner. It was then laid and secured by the builder.

Originating in 1871 when the Reverend Samuel Edwards came to Cañon City once a month, the Christ Episcopal Church congregation met in Murray's Hall above the saloon and later Bate's Hall until 1876, when a church building was erected. The cornerstone was laid, and several items were enclosed in it, including a Holy Bible, the Book of Common Prayer, copies of local newspapers, and excerpts from a historical address given by Anson Rudd at the centennial July 4, 1876, celebration to Cañon City citizens.

Built as a home in 1913 on Fifteenth Street for sick and indigent members of the Independent Order of Odd Fellows, the lovely stone building remains today. The Odd Fellows organization dates to the 14th century in the United Kingdom and was comprised of members of various tradesman's guilds that came together to aid members in need. The beautiful home on North Fifteenth Street also was an orphanage for many children in the city.

Elks Temple Canon City Colo.

Through the years, many civic-minded groups, such as the Benevolent and Protective Order of Elks, have called Cañon City home. The Cañon City Elks lodge was instituted on the evening of July 30, 1900, in Shaeffer Hall at 426–428 Main Street. "Despite its youth the local Elks Lodge is one of the leading social and benevolent orders of our city, and its members confidently look forward to a better future for it in good works and helpful action in behalf of those needing and deserving aid," reported the July 3, 1902, *Cañon City Record*.

Women have always been active in Cañon City social groups, as shown in this photograph of the Women's Reading Club. A December 22, 1899, *Cañon City Clipper* editorial defends women's clubs at the time "There is a vast difference between women's clubs and men's clubs. There is a loud smell of champagne, beer, tobacco smoke and poker around the average men's club, illuminated now and then with prize fights, variety actresses, and orgies of a doubtful character. The women however have a different notion of clubs. Theirs is purely educational."

Bicycling was a favorite pastime of early Cañon City residents. The *Cañon City Daily Record* reported that Pres. Grover Cleveland declared, "Women past first blush of youth and beauty have no business to ride a wheel." The March 19, 1896, *Cañon City Daily Record* stated, "We hope our lady readers of this class outside of Colorado will take heed and give up this vulgar practice." Then the newspaper continued on with a tongue-in-cheek remark, stating, "Women who live in the congenial clime and balmy atmosphere of Colorado never pass the first blush of youth and beauty."

Six

CRIME AND PUNISHMENT

Numerous lynchings, including that of George Witherell on December 4, 1888, colored early Cañon City history. Frontier justice caught up with Witherell at a light pole on the corner of First and Main Streets where the armory now stands. Notice the territorial prison in the background. Witherell allegedly murdered rancher Charles McCain and was captured in Denver. A vigilante mob forced Sheriff Morgan L. Griffith to hand over Witherell. They marched him down the street and hanged him.

The Prospect Heights Jail, known for being a rough place to visit, is located in what used to be the town of Prospect Heights on the south side of Cañon City. It was determined that the jail was needed to house lawbreakers and dry out patrons (usually coal miners) of the eight lively bars operating in the two-block area of town. During the silent film days, actor Tom Mix was a visitor to the jail when a night of drinking got out of hand.

A much-needed territorial prison, "Old Max," shown in the foreground, was built in Cañon City in 1871 several years before Colorado became a state. The frontier was wild and brawling, and jails were often filled to capacity. Law officers of the region were frustrated when there was no place to put convicted criminals, so hangings or acquittals were frequently the only options. City attorney Thomas Macon spearheaded the effort to bring the prison to Cañon City.

Growth came fast to the Colorado State Penitentiary, as this 1890 photograph shows. Prison overcrowding has always been a real problem for the United States, and at the date of this writing, there are now over 13 prison facilities, both state and federal, in the Cañon City area.

Prison life, while generally unpleasant, has moments of lightheartedness. Through the years, prisons have had baseball teams, prison bands, plays, and movies. As shown in this January 1, 1934, minstrel show photograph, traveling entertainers also came to perform for the inmates.

Female inmates were housed just outside of the east gate of the penitentiary in an updated women's facility built in 1935, which now houses the Colorado Museum of Prisons. A modern women's prison was completed in 1968 at the east end of Cañon City, where it housed and educated woman for over 40 years. The Colorado Women's Correctional Facility closed in 2009 due to state budget cuts.

The female department building was finished in 1909 with funds appropriated by the State of Colorado for housing patients suffering with tuberculosis and insanity. The women were taught life skills, such as sewing, child care, cooking, and cosmetology.

Colorado law stated that wardens for the penitentiary were required to live on the grounds, and that also included their families. Warden E. H. Martin's family was no exception, as his daughter is shown in this photograph from about 1900 in the front yard. The east gate in the prison wall is shown behind her. Over 20 inmate trustees maintained the home and grounds and even cooked, cleaned, babysat, and chauffeured for the families until the last residing warden, Wayne K. Patterson, left in 1972.

Built in 1901 at 105 Main Street to house the deputy warden and his family, the home featured a full basement and was heated by steam from the prison boilers located on the other side of the prison walls. This Queen Anne–style home was designed by C. C. Rittenhouse, who was the architect for many of the buildings and homes in the city. The home replaced the Fremont House, or Fremont Hotel, which had stood at that location since the early 1860s.

From the beginning of the prison to the 1950s, the "Old Grey Mare" was used to discipline unruly inmates. The prisoner was strapped and handcuffed over the beam, and then a long, wide leather strap dipped in water induced an attitude adjustment.

Warden Roy Best, a famous and flamboyant warden serving from 1932 to 1952, was a strict disciplinarian, and whenever inmates were out of their cells they were to have their arms folded in front of them. His philosophy was that no inmate should ever be idle, an idea that would later cause him quite a lot of legal trouble. Many work and recreation programs were started under his watch. Notice the two Doberman pinschers, Chris and Ike, at the warden's side; both dogs are buried at the prison in the prison dog cemetery.

Always trying to improve things on his watch, Best brought the first gas chamber in 1932 to the penitentiary, as well as the electric eye, an early metal detector that monitored inmates as they came in from working outside of the prison.

Prison guards held hostage were killed one by one by inmate No. 14277, Danny Daniels, in Cell House 3 during the October 3, 1929, riot because ransom demands for vehicles in which to escape were not met by Warden F. E. Crawford. As Cell House 1 burned, seen here, Daniels killed the other inmates who helped him incite the riot, then he killed himself so no one would be hung after the gruesome and dreadful day.

A testament to the fallen officers of the fiery and violent 1929 riot that nearly destroyed the prison grounds and many buildings, hearses are prepared to remove the bodies of the eight brave guards killed that day in the line of duty. Several more officers were wounded, including Crawford, who received buckshot from a stray round into his chest and forehead.

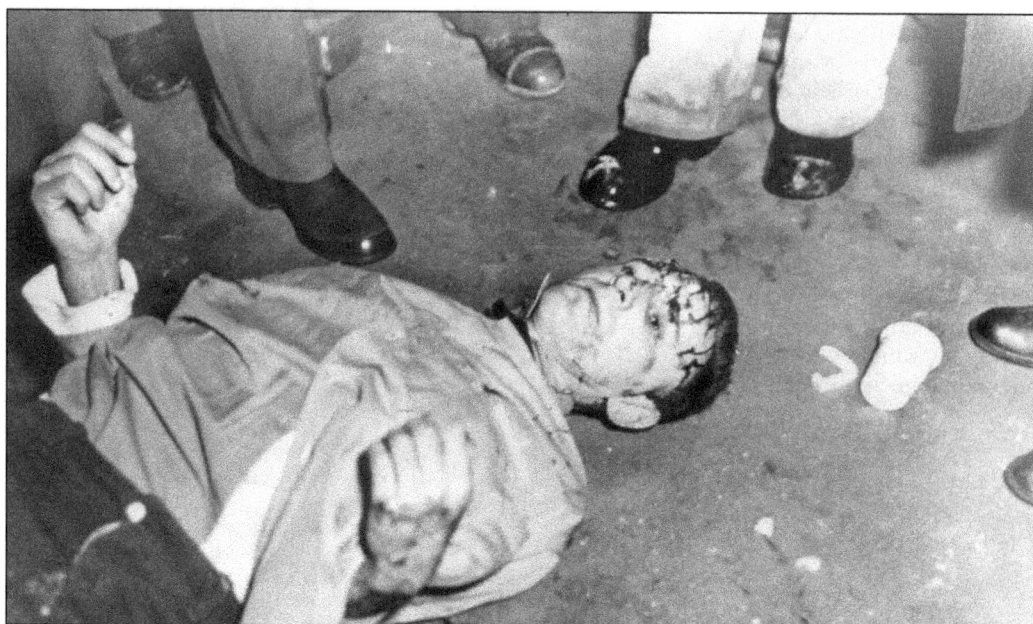

A December 30, 1947, prison break became famous after the world premier movie *Cañon City* was made. One of the actual escapees, Werner Schwartzmiller, was holding rancher Mr. Oliver and his wife hostage at their home. Seeing her opportunity, brave Mrs. Oliver grabbed a claw hammer and struck Schwartzmiller on the head and shoulder, and her husband, Lawrence Oliver, and a guard who was also being held hostage tied him up for capture.

During the escape of December 30, 1947, inmates Orville Turley and Richard Heilman made their way toward the town of Florence, where they holed up in a small trailer house. The owner of the trailer cowered under the bed while the two escapees were told to come out of the trailer by a posse. When they refused, the posse opened fire and Turley was mortally wounded, while Heilman (left) received a head wound and surrendered.

Colorado's most famous cannibal, Alferd Packer, was sentenced in 1874 for the killing and cannibalism of five prospectors during an expedition from Pennsylvania to Colorado that he was hired to lead. When Packer was the only one to come out of the mountains close to Saguache in the spring looking well fed and healthy, people started to wonder what became of his companions. Packer served much of his sentence for manslaughter in Cañon City and was paroled in 1901.

The sensational murder of Leo Hutchinson at the hands of his quiet wife, Stella Hutchinson, in the Lincoln Park area caught the attention of Cañon City residents in 1948. Leo reportedly abused and threatened his wife for more than 23 years, and after a lengthy argument, she pulled a .38 out of the kitchen dumbwaiter and shot him several times.

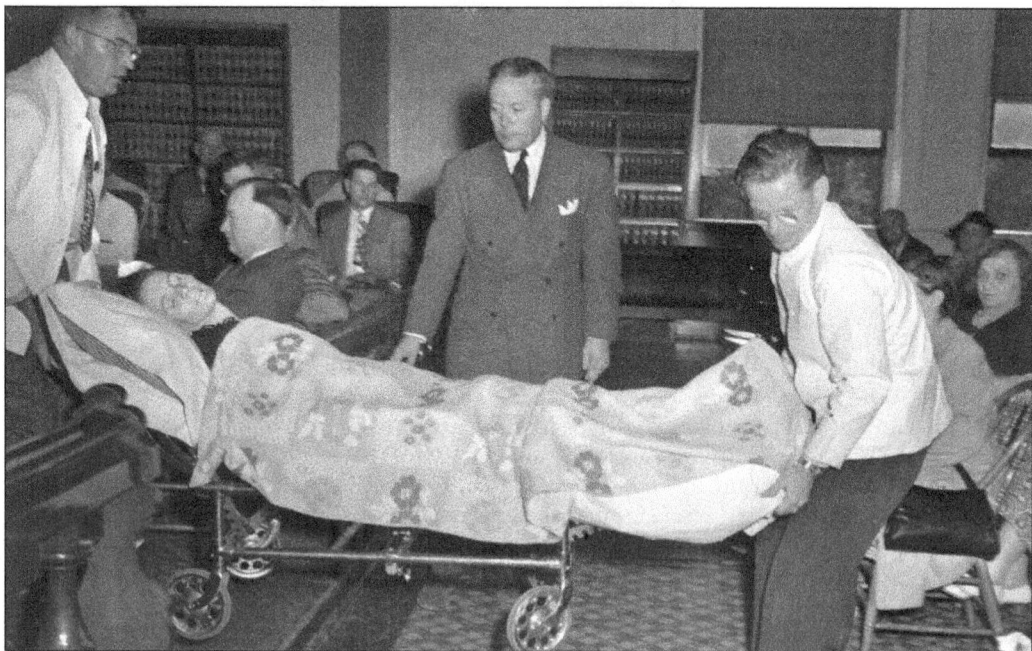

Stella collapsed in court as her trial progressed. The prosecutor was showing the bloody clothing her husband wore when she killed him. The trial ended with Stella being acquitted in a self-defense ruling and was quoted in the *Cañon City Daily Record* as saying, "Certainly I killed him . . . I don't have any regrets."

Seven

ON LOCATION

The Selig Polyscope Company and the Colorado Motion Picture Company were two of the earliest film companies in the country. This photograph from about 1914 shows the Colorado Motion Picture Company building at the southwest corner of Third and Main Streets. The film crew is getting ready for a long day of shooting. Actress Josephine West is seated on her horse, while O. B. Thayer, the company's director and producer, is standing on the left running board of the vehicle.

This dramatic scene shows Josephine West in *Pirates of the Plains* surrounded by concerned cowboys while kneeling over her dead horse. Two of the cowboys are wearing wool chaps and several are mounted. The animal is thought to be from the string of horses provided by Charlie Reeves, a local who also acted in several silent films.

The heroine West races to save her man in the 1914 silent film *Pirates of the Plains*. Bud Chase is about to hang for a murder he did not commit, while Thayer stands by as the priest. The hangman set was built at the Colorado State Penitentiary, as shown by guard tower No. 4 in the background. The Colorado State Penitentiary was the location for several films, including the 1967 movie *In Cold Blood*, starring John Forsythe.

Early silent films were wrought with accidents, injuries, and death. *Across the Border*, a film about gunrunning along the United States–Mexican border during the Mexican Revolution, was one of the last films made in Cañon City. On July 1, 1914, lovely Grace McHugh and cameraman Owen Carter were drowned in the Arkansas River while reshooting a scene close to the Hot Springs Hotel. Her body was recovered two weeks later near Florence.

Cañon City locals were frequently used as extras in the films shot in the area and were paid around $5 per day. John P. (Jack) Donahoo, shown here in a movie arresting two felons, came to Cañon City with the Selig Polyscope Company and starred in several Westerns. When the motion picture companies moved from the area, Donahoo stayed and became the undersheriff and later the Cañon City chief of police.

Movie locations in the Cañon City area include Buckskin Joe, Tunnel Drive, Brush Hollow Reservoir, Red Canyon Park, Old Max territorial prison, the Royal Gorge Canyon, the Rudd stone house, Grape Creek, and the Giem Ranch on High Park Road.

In 1948, Cañon City was host to the world premier movie *Cañon City* about the real prison break that made headlines in December 1947. Not one to shy away from publicity, warden Roy Best played himself, and many local citizens were used as extras. This scene shows Best surrounded by reporters and officers getting ready to head out to track down the escaped felons.

One scene in *Cañon City* depicted James Sherbondy, who used a crude, homemade shotgun to hold the Bauer family hostage, while Mrs. Mary Lou Bauer was ordered to make the convict a plate of eggs. The Bauer children were ill at the time, with little Jerry Bauer suffering from appendicitis. Mrs. Bauer was allowed to take them to the doctor. Later Sherbondy was captured just outside of the home, showing the exciting climax of the real escape, as well as the movie.

Mrs. Lonnie Higgens and Mrs. Lawrence Oliver were flown to New York to tell their stories of heroism from the 1946 prison break. Part of the publicity for the *Cañon City* film was their broadcast from New York on the CBS *We the People* show.

Cañon City–area beauty queens Joan Tyner, Helen Wildgren, and Jeannie Camerlo, shown with escort "Doc" Little, made an eventful trip on Monarch Airlines's "Roy Best, Cañon City Premier Special" to Hollywood to escort the film home to Cañon City for the world premier.

From left to right, Warden Roy Best is seen on his big day by the theater marquee with actor Scott Brady, who portrayed inmate James Sherbondy. They are standing with Colorado governor W. Lee Knous, Sen. Edwin C. Johnson, and former governor Ralph Carr. The children in town wore shirts striped with electrical tape to show off the prison theme.

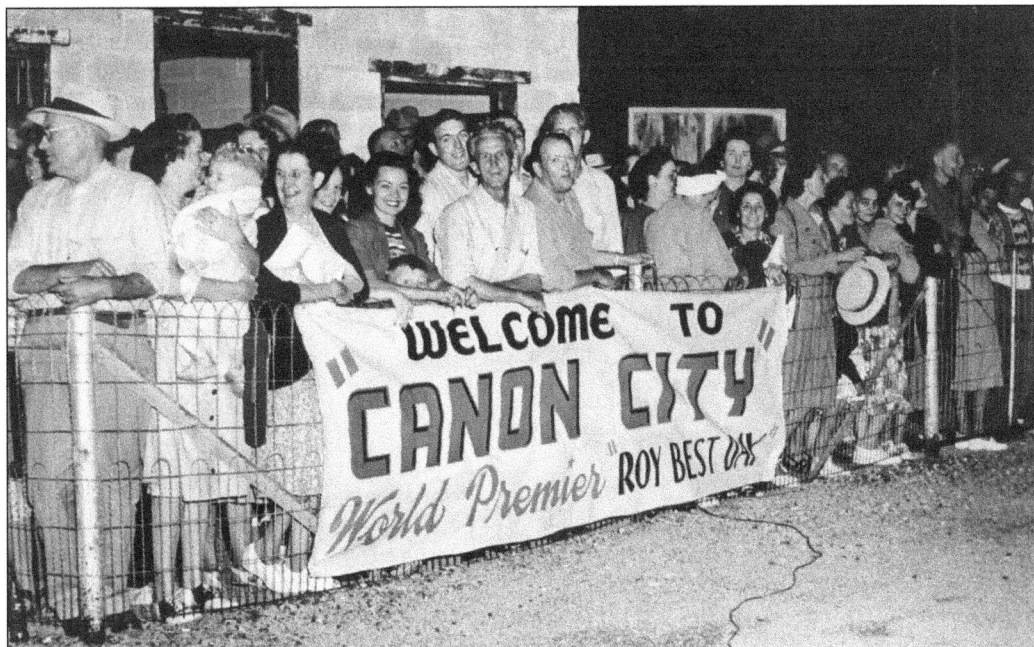

Hundreds of *Cañon City* movie fans line up for a glimpse of screen stars and dignitaries at the Fremont County Airport. VIP–invited world premier ticket holders viewed a special presentation from within the prison itself on what was dubbed Roy Best Day, in honor of the famous prison warden.

Premiering in Cañon City and Florence on February 6, 1951, *Vengeance Valley* starred Hugh O'Brien, real-life newlyweds Joanne Dru and John Ireland, and Burt Lancaster. They stayed in Cañon City as the film was made. Swarms of local bobby-soxers invaded the Cañon Hotel, hoping to catch a glimpse of Lancaster and the other stars.

One scene for the movie *The Cowboys*, showing John Wayne as Wil Andersen riding his big sorrel horse down the street, was filmed at Buckskin Joe in 1972. *The Cowboys* was supposed to be filmed entirely in Cañon City, but a mix-up with the cattle forced the film to move to another location. Wayne was only able to stay in the area for a few hours.

98

The 1977 film *White Buffalo* was directed by J. Lee Thompson. It starred Charles Bronson as Wild Bill Hickock and Will Sampson as Crazy Horse and featured Jack Warden, Clint Walker, and Slim Pickens. It was filmed in the Cañon City area and was about a white buffalo that Hickock dreamed about hunting.

Gus and Doris Salardino welcomed many entertainers to their Sali's Paradise restaurant just west of Ninth Street over the years. Kerwin Matthews, Gus Salardino, and Mariette Hartley share a laugh while taking a break from working on *Barquero*, which was filmed on location at Brush Hollow Reservoir in Penrose in 1969.

A scene from the film *The Duchess and the Dirtwater Fox*, with Goldie Hawn and George Segal, is shown in this photograph. The lively, bawdy Western was shot at Buckskin Joe and other Cañon City locations, including the historical Rudd stone house in 1975.

The 1978 ABC made-for-television movie *True Grit*, starring Warren Oates, Lisa Pelikan, and Lee Meriweather, was based on the John Wayne character from the original 1969 movie of the same name. The location of the set was the Grape Creek area.

Eight

THEY MADE A DIFFERENCE

"People living today simply cannot realize what it cost to civilize Colorado," said Truman Blancett, one of the last Native American scouts alive, in an interview dated September 28, 1939. Blancett knew many of the outstanding figures of the West, including Kit Carson, Buffalo Bill, and Chief Ouray. He was instrumental in establishing wagon trails between government forts and early pioneer settlements. Blancett was over 100 years old at the time of his death in Cañon City in 1945.

Colorful sportsman, developer, and dam builder, Dallas (Dall) DeWeese made huge contributions to Cañon City. A visionary, DeWeese saw great opportunity in the town when he purchased 1,800 acres, put in orchards, and then began selling three- to five-acre parcels. Engineering the DeWeese Reservoir in Custer County to irrigate the land he was selling proved to be a brilliant financial move by turning dry, arid land into fertile farmland enticing thousands of people to the city.

A friend and contemporary of Pres. Theodore Roosevelt, DeWeese was an extremely successful big-game hunter. While in Alaska in 1898, he noted that there was far less game there than one year earlier and sent a letter to Roosevelt to begin game preservation by way of hunting laws and game preserves nationally. He is shown in this photograph with his moose.

The DeWeese lodge was built of logs and was called "the shack" by DeWeese. It stood for over 100 years until destroyed by fire in January 2007. The lodge was a two-story log home hand built mostly by DeWeese. Rustic on the outside, the lodge had every convenience of the time. He had the mounts from all of his hunting adventures hung around the 24-by-24-foot den. DeWeese and his wife loved to entertain in their home, hosting great parties during the annual Fruit Day celebrations.

Mild weather made Cañon City a favorite wintering ground for the Tabeguache Ute Indian tribes, including their famous chief, Ouray and his beautiful wife, Chipeta. Camping close to the hot springs, they traded often with the growing white community. Ouray worked tirelessly to improve relations between the settlers and the Native American tribes traveling to Washington, D.C., several times with a delegation. His last visit to Cañon City was in 1876 to see Dr. J. F. Lewis, where he was diagnosed with a kidney disease.

Born in 1852 as the youngest of 17 children, James H. Peabody moved to Cañon City in 1875 to work for James Clelland in his mercantile store, eventually becoming a partner in the firm. Peabody became the Fremont County clerk and held that office while organizing the First National Bank of Cañon City, becoming its president in 1891. He became widely known in the state as an active Republican and was nominated governor in 1902. Widespread labor troubles marred his administration, and a mining war between the Western Mining Federation of Miners and the mine owners ended up with violence in 1904. Peabody ran for a second term, won, and resigned immediately. He retired to Cañon City, where he lived the rest of his life.

Peabody (center, in the dark costume) performed the lead role in *The Mikado* soon after his return to Cañon City. The highly popular play was written by W. S. Gilbert and Arthur Sullivan in 1885. It was performed around 1905 by several people from Cañon City for the enjoyment of its residents at the opera house in the 600 block of Main Street, where the Skyline Theater parking lot sits presently.

Learning his craft during World War II in the intelligence section of Adm. R. K. Turner's staff, Karol Smith photographed landing operations such as those at Iwo Jima with the Marine Corps while working as a liaison between Turner and the joint chiefs of staff. After Smith finished with his military service, he came home to Cañon City and worked as a photographer for the *Cañon City Daily Record* and was also retained by the *Denver Post*. His photographs chronicled decades of Cañon City events until his death in 1992.

Directly involved with the movie industry, beginning with the film *Cañon City* in which producers used his photographs from the actual prison break in 1947, Karol Smith was also responsible for building the Buckskin Joe area for use as a movie set and tourist attraction. In the late 1960s, Smith and Sen. Harold McCormick lobbied to establish a state agency to promote Colorado for location filming of motion pictures and television programs. Smith was its director until his retirement in 1989. This photograph shows Smith at Buckskin Joe with John Wayne during the filming of the promotion portion of *The Cowboys*.

Harold McCormick grew up in the Cañon City area involved with his family's theater chain. He spent World War II with the Eighth Air Force in England attached to the 14th Bomb Group as a photographer. When the war ended, he came home to Cañon City where he became a senator in 1960 and served almost 30 years in the Colorado state legislature. McCormick was instrumental in building the Women's Prison facility in Cañon City, improving water monitoring of the rivers in the state, and helping to establish the Colorado Film Commission, the nation's oldest.

Led by Fred Arnold, minister of the First Baptist Church at Seventh and Macon Streets, the Ku Klux Klan had a short-lived influence in the early 1920s when Cañon City became the state headquarters for the group. Protesting the influx of Catholics and European immigrants, they caused quite a stir in the mining towns surrounding Cañon City. With their own newspaper and meeting place in the Hotel Cañon, several influential city members were involved for short time. When B. F. Rockefellow sold much of his Fruitmere orchard land to the Catholic Church to build the Holy Cross Abbey, it proved that the Ku Klux Klan was not welcomed by many in the community.

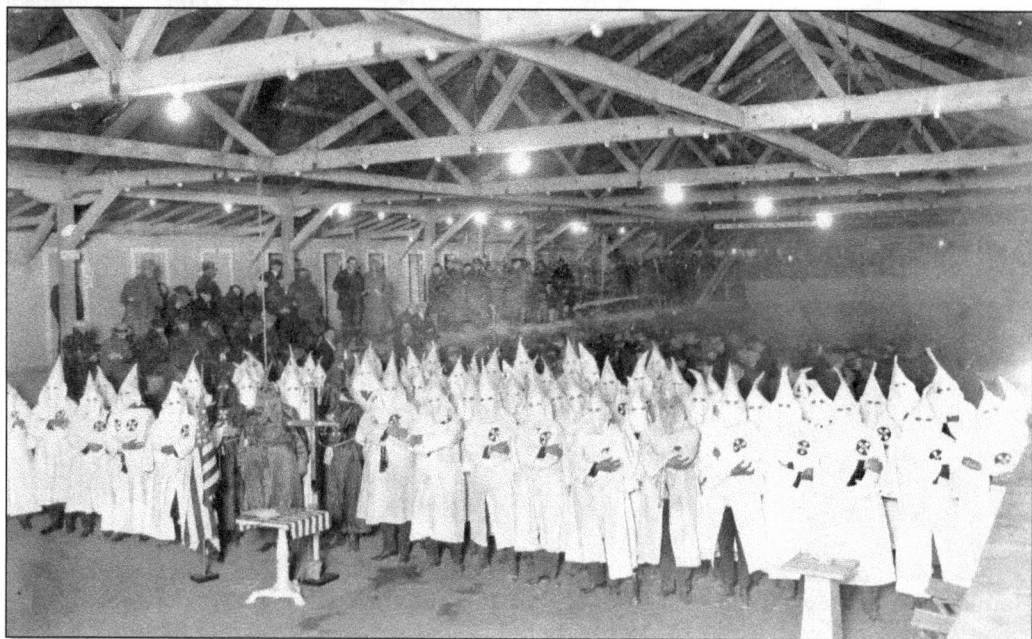

Frightening parades and cross burnings marked the Ku Klux Klan's short-lived presence in Cañon City. Shown in this photograph is the Ku Klux Klan during the January 26, 1924, debut of Klan Charter No. 21, with almost 500 members in an elaborate ceremony led by the Grand Dragon at the Natatorium swimming pool east of town where Central Avenue and Dozier Avenue meet.

Many local political races became hotly contested when Klansmen ran for office in 1924 and candidates won several races. This advertisement showed an obvious support for the Klan by the owner of this business for the "invisible empire." The Klan moved on from Cañon City after Rev. Fred Arnold lost his son in an accident and moved to Denver.

During the late 1800s, Dyke F. Engleman and his wife, Jennie, thrilled Cañon City residents with their amazing feats on the high-wire. They worked under the stage name of Millman and Millman, a blending of his grandfather's name Milton Engleman. This photograph is presumably of Dyke's high-wire above Main Street in front of the McClure House Hotel. Later Dyke and Jennie added their tiny daughter Jennadean to their act, making them the Millman Trio, where they performed for small circuses across the country.

Lovely, diminutive Jennadean Engleman of the Millman Trio was nicknamed "Bird" for her size and the way she danced, whirled, and pirouetted across the high-wire. Quickly overshadowing her parents' act by the time she was 12, she was a sensation with her solo act. She signed with Ringling Brothers in 1913 and performed with the circus, as well as the Zigfield Follies, where she performed her wire act high atop the New Amsterdam roof. She died in 1940 after moving home several years earlier to Cañon City.

Sent to Colorado as a young man for his health in 1893, Guy U. Hardy found a job as reporter for the *Cañon City Record* and eventually took over the newspaper from A. R. Frisbee in 1895. Hardy built the newspaper to become the number one source for news in the area. After his election to Congress, Hardy worked to defeat the Ku Klux Klan and also to secure the land surrounding the Royal Gorge Bridge, Temple Canyon, and Red Canyon Park as properties of the city.

Born in 1879 in a log cabin on a ranch on Currant Creek, Robert Wesley Amick attended local Cañon City schools and learned to sketch the West of his youth. After acquiring a law degree at Yale College, Amick gave up law to study art, becoming a highly respected Western artist. His paintings have been used in multiple books chronicling ranch life. He also painted the mural in the Royal Gorge Regional Museum and History Center when it was built in 1927.

Raised in Cañon City, Rear Adm. Emory S. Land (shown on the left in this photograph with Joe Kennedy) went to the U.S. Naval Academy at Annapolis and had a stellar athletic career there, earning the Athletic Sword upon graduation. Land was awarded the Navy Cross for his technical studies of German submarines in World War I. Tough-minded and determined, Land was named chairman of the Maritime Commission by Pres. Franklin D. Roosevelt in 1937 and was a driving force in building the U.S. Navy fleet with more than 4,000 Liberty and Victory ships, feeling that trouble was brewing abroad. The USS *Emory S. Land* (AS 39) was named for him, as well as Land Mountain 3 miles southwest of Cañon City.

Reared in the Independent Order of Odd Fellows orphanage, Jack Christiansen was shot in the arm by a Canon City police officer in 1945 during a high school prank. With his shattered arm, Jack thought his football career was over. He went on to Colorado Agricultural and Mechanical College (now Colorado State University) and ran track. During his sophomore year, he tried out for the football team and went on to a successful college career. Christiansen was drafted by the Detroit Lions in 1951 and went on to set many records, mostly as a punt returner. He was inducted into the Pro Football Hall of Fame in 1970. (Courtesy Jack Christiansen, 1950 University Historic Photograph Collection, Colorado State University, Archives and Special Collections.)

Nine

MINING

While Cañon City was not a huge gold mining draw itself, the major gold and silver towns surrounding Cañon City from Cripple Creek and Victor to the north, Leadville and Fairplay to the west, and Silver Cliff to the south, made Cañon City the ideal hub for supplies and commerce for the prospectors of the gold rush days. H. A. W. Tabor and others floated railroad ties through Cañon City on the Arkansas River to further construction of the railroad lines crossing the state.

Hundreds of coal mines, much like the Wolf Park Mine of the Cañon City Reliance Fuel Company around 1940, dotted the early landscape of Cañon City and throughout Fremont County. Started by the Littell Brothers in the 1890s, Wolf Park's mine shaft was said to be the deepest in the state at 1,029 feet. Railroad cars from the Atchison, Topeka, and Santa Fe Railway sit ready for the different grades of coal to be loaded and shipped.

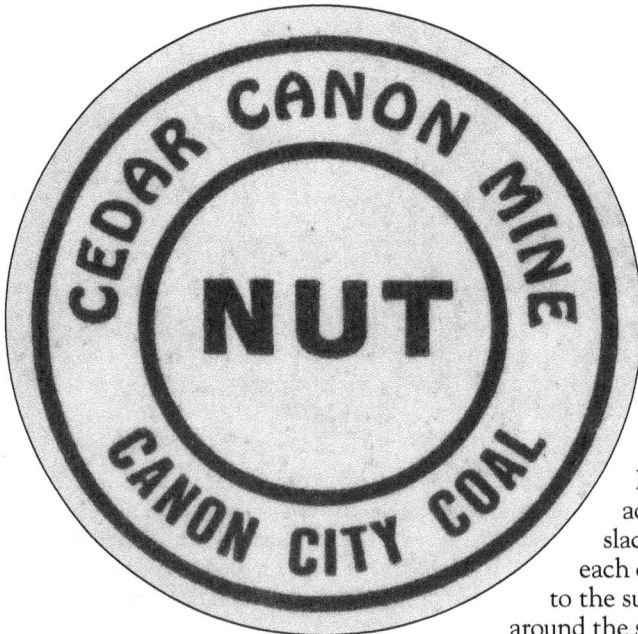

This coal token from Cedar Cañon Mine was used in sorting the coal according to size and quality—lump, slack, chestnut, and so forth. Placed atop each coal car, it would be sorted as it went to the surface and then sent to communities around the state.

Taken around 1881, this photograph shows the American Mining and Smelting Company on the east side of South Ninth Street near the Arkansas River. This smelter used a water wheel to power the crusher and other equipment, which eventually caused the downstream community trouble and thus the demise of the business. Later the U.S. Smelting and Refining Company in Prospect Heights took over most of the ore business until about 1909.

VIEW FROM NORTH EAST

Seen in this photograph from around 1917, more than 100 men were employed at the Empire Zinc Plant, placing it as one the leading contributors to the Cañon City–area economy of the time. The Empire Zinc Plant in South Cañon handled ores from as far away as Leadville and other surrounding mining towns to be used for a variety of products, such as spark plug covers, motor housings, ornamental boxes, die castings, and furniture decoration.

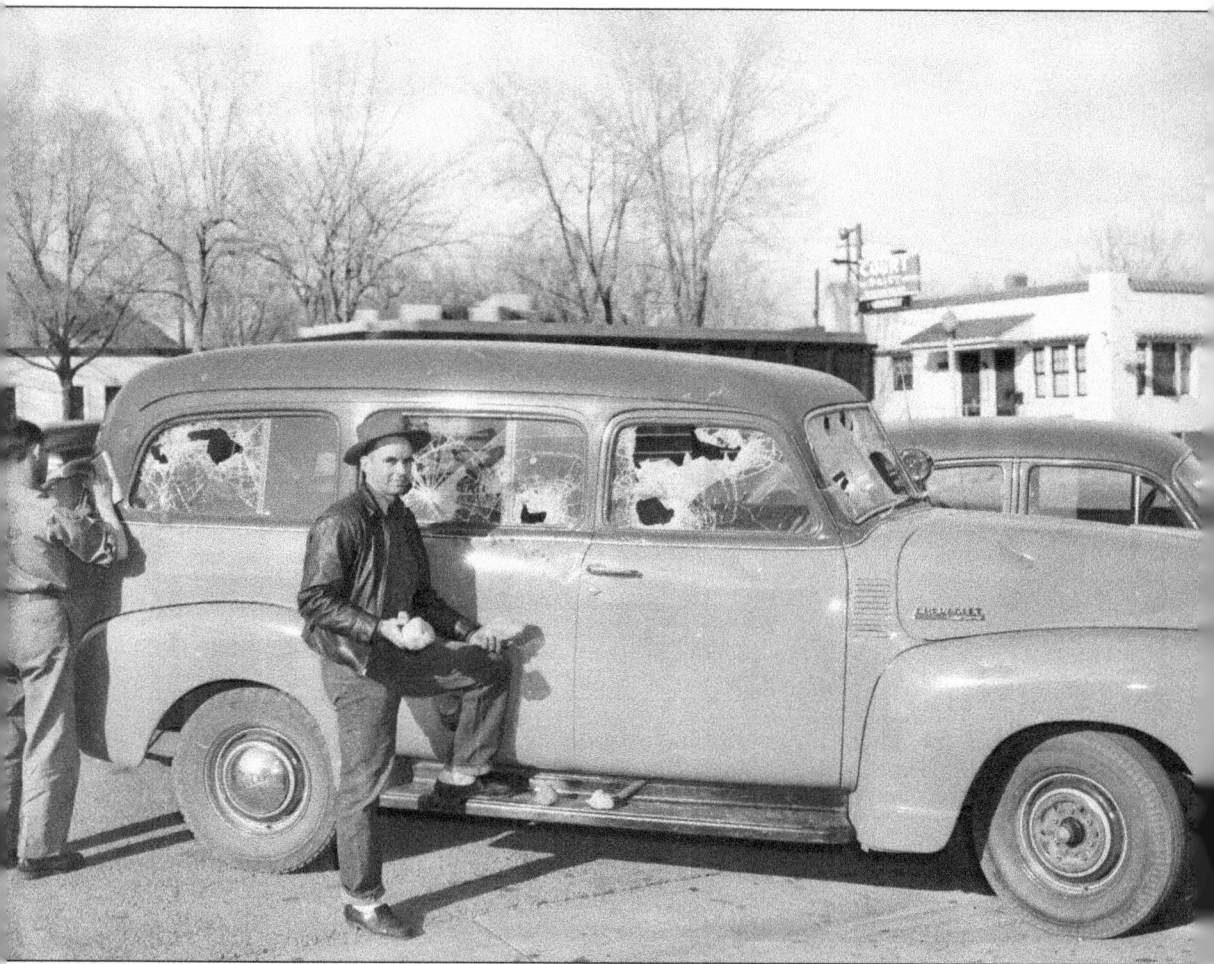

Coal mining was an extremely dangerous job and strikes were frequent. Several violent strikes made history when clashes related to unionizing the miners heated up. The Ludlow Massacre of April 20, 1914, taking place north of Trinidad, in which 19 men, women, and children were killed by soldiers of the Colorado National Guard, made national headlines and created grave tension in the Cañon City area mines. A gunfight between the coal company and the striking miners occurred, where one miner was shot in the head bringing federal troops to Cañon City. It caused the longest trial in the county at the time. This photograph shows damage to a vehicle during a strike in 1950.

The Chandler Mine, owned by the Western Fuel Company and later by the Victor-American Company, employed around 300 men in the 1920s and was known in the industry for its lasting clean burning and heating qualities. The mine was equipped with boilers, electric machinery, and every modern mining apparatus. The Victor-American Company boasted the mine was the finest in Fremont County.

Miners spent much of their time underground, but when time allowed, they loved to play baseball, creating intense rivalries between mining camps. Games were played on Sunday afternoons, with everyone in town in attendance. Chandler miners even had their own sand-greens golf course north of town. During Prohibition, home-brewed beer was enjoyed, and in between innings, fans reportedly scrambled home for a quick drink.

The mine shaft was deep, dark, and damp, and company mules lived deep inside of the mine never to see the light of day. Boys as young as 10 years old, as well as old men, destroyed their backs and lungs bent over in cramped mine tunnels for hours and days on end to earn meager incomes with which to feed their families. Most mines did not have any sort of compensation for medical expenses, and if a miner died, it was up to the other miners to take care of the family of the deceased.

Running the mine hoist was a noisy job that required skill and concentration but one that also allowed a man to see the light of day. The miners depended on the hoist to get supplies down to them and ore out of the deep mine shaft. This man is working for the Hastings Victor Fuel Company. Notice the heavy cable used for the steam-powered hoist.

When the Chandler Mine opened in 1890, it created a company town platted with 11 blocks, a schoolhouse, a boardinghouse, a saloon, and a company store but no churches. A company town meant that only those with mine business could live in the tidy little community. Chandler prospered until the mine closed in 1942, and nothing remains except a few stone foundations.

Said to be the prettiest mining town in Fremont County, Chandler homes were neat and landscaped, and the streets were kept clean. The schoolhouse was the center for all of the town functions, and children's plays and Christmas programs were attended by all.

Rockvale, southeast of Cañon City, was a booming town at its peak, with a town band, a first aid team that competed around the region, a highly competitive baseball team, a YMCA, a grocery store, and a stage that made the rounds between the mining camps. Rockvale boasted 13 saloons, and Gus Salardino and his brothers opened the Gold Nugget Night Club and hosted the most talented and popular entertainers of the 1930s and 1940s.

Rockvale miners hastily hid more than 50 wives and children in a large cave outside of town during the labor wars of 1913 and 1914. Tensions were high after the Ludlow Massacre in April 1914 and because federal troops camped at the edge of town, and it was feared that shooting would start at any moment. However, cool heads prevailed, and there were no injuries at Rockvale at that time.

The Radiant Mine opened in 1903 just 3 miles south of Coal Creek and was another Victor-American Fuel Company establishment. The company built around 80 homes with no modern facilities for heat or plumbing. A boardinghouse for Italians was built in 1906, as well as a company store, a saloon, and a two-room schoolhouse.

During the Depression, the Radiant Mine closed, leaving several homes standing vacant. The federal government needed homes for the many transients roaming the country looking for employment. Radiant was turned into a Federal Emergency Relief Administration camp and, later, when economic conditions eased, the camp was closed and the homes sold and relocated.

Here is a Radiant home being relocated to another Fremont County town after it was sold at auction in the late 1930s. The company store was donated to the American Legion, and it became the Florence Eagle's Hall.

Beautiful rock has been quarried in the Cañon City area for over 100 years. Travertine, conglomerate, high-quality marble, and many precious and semiprecious gems, such as amethyst, topaz, and turquoise, are found in the mountains outside of the city.

Colorado building stones are divided into five classes or grades: granite, marble, limestone, sandstone, and lava. Terrazzo, an Italian word, is made out of chips of travertine, marble, and other stones mixed with cement, poured, and buffed to create a highly polished, very durable and beautiful surface.

Royal Breche marble, quarried from Fremont County and polished, was used to build the Fremont County Courthouse, located at 615 Macon Street. Travertine, conglomerate, and marble from Fremont County have been used to construct buildings in many U.S. cities, including the Colorado State Capital, the Lincoln Memorial, and the Tomb of the Unknowns at Arlington National Cemetery.

Visit us at
arcadiapublishing.com

···